FOLLOWING
CHRIST,
NO MATTER
THE COST

Contents

Welcome

WE ARE GLAD you have decided to join us in this Bible study! First of all, please know that you have been prayed for! It is not a coincidence you are participating in this study.

Our prayer for you is simple: that you will grow closer to our Lord as you dig into His Word each and every day! As you develop the discipline of being in God's Word on a daily basis, our prayer is that you will fall in love with Him even more as you spend time reading from the Bible.

Each day before you read the assigned scripture(s), pray and ask God to help you understand it. Invite Him to speak to you through His Word. Then listen. It's His job to speak to you, and it's your job to listen and obey.

Take time to read the verses over and over again. We are told in Proverbs to search and you will find: "Search for it like silver, and hunt for it like hidden treasure. Then you will understand" (Prov. 2:4–5 NCV).

We are thrilled to provide these different resources for you as you participate in our online Bible study:

- *Sold Out - Following Christ, No Matter the Cost* Study Journal
- Reading Plan
- Weekly Blog Posts (Mondays, Wednesdays, and Fridays)
- Weekly Memory Verses
- Weekly Monday Videos
- Weekly Challenges
- Online Community: Facebook, Twitter, Instagram, LoveGodGreatly.com
- Hashtags: #LoveGodGreatly

All of us here at Love God Greatly can't wait for you to get started, and we hope to see you at the finish line. Endure, persevere, press on—and don't give up! Finish well what you are beginning today. We will be here every step of the way, cheering you on! We are in this together. Fight to rise early, to push back the stress of the day, to sit alone and spend time in God's Word! Let's see what God has in store for you in this study! Journey with us as we learn to love God greatly with our lives!

Our Community

LOVE GOD GREATLY (LGG) is a beautiful community of women who use a variety of technology platforms to keep each other accountable in God's Word.

We start with a simple Bible reading plan, but it doesn't stop there.

Some women gather in homes and churches locally, while others connect online with women across the globe. Whatever the method, we lovingly lock arms and unite for this purpose: to love God greatly with our lives.

In today's fast-paced technology-driven world, it would be easy to study God's Word in an isolated environment that lacks encouragement or support, but that isn't the intention here at Love God Greatly. God created us to live in community with Him and with those around us.

We need each other, and we live life better together.

Because of this, would you consider reaching out and doing this study with someone?

All of us have women in our lives who need friendship, accountability, and have the desire to dive into God's Word on a deeper level. Rest assured we'll be studying right alongside you—learning with you, cheering for you, enjoying sweet fellowship, and smiling from ear to ear as we watch God unite women together—intentionally connecting hearts and minds for His glory.

It's pretty unreal, this opportunity we have to grow not only closer to God through this study but also to each other. So here's the challenge: call your mom, your sister, your grandma, the girl across the street, or the college friend across the country. Gather a group of girls from your church or workplace, or meet in a coffee shop with friends you have always wished you knew better. Utilize the beauty of connecting online for inspiration and accountability, and take opportunities to meet in person when you can.

Arm-in-arm and hand-in-hand, let's do this thing...together.

How to SOAP

WE'RE PROUD OF YOU.

We really want you to know that.

We're proud of you for making the commitment to be in God's Word, to be reading it each day and applying it to your life, the beautiful life our Lord has given you.

In this study we offer you a study journal to accompany the verses we are reading. This journal is designed to help you interact with God's Word and learn to dig deeper, encouraging you to slow down and reflect on what God is saying to you that day.

At Love God Greatly, we use the SOAP Bible study method. Before beginning, let's take a moment to define this method and share why we recommend using it during your quiet time.

Why SOAP It?

It's one thing to simply read Scripture. But when you interact with it, intentionally slowing down to really reflect on it, suddenly words start popping off the page. The SOAP method allows you to dig deeper into Scripture and see more than you would if you simply read the verses and then went on your merry way. Please take the time to SOAP through our Bible studies and see for yourself how much more you get from your daily reading. You'll be amazed.

What Does SOAP Mean?

S stands for **Scripture**. Physically write out the verses. You'll be amazed at what God will reveal to you just by taking the time to slow down and write out what you are reading!

O stands for **observation**. What do you see in the verses that you're reading? Who is the intended audience? Is there a repetition of words? What words stand out to you?

A stands for **application**. This is when God's Word becomes personal. What is God saying to you today? How can you apply what you just read to your own personal life? What changes do you need to make? Is there action you need to take?

P stands for **prayer**. Pray God's Word back to Him. Spend time thanking Him. If He has revealed something to you during this time in His Word, pray about it. If He has revealed some sin that is in your life, confess. And remember, He loves you dearly.

Follow This Example

Scripture: Read and write out Colossians 1:5–8.

> "The faith and love that spring from the hope stored up for you in heaven and about which you have already heard in the true message of the gospel that has come to you. In the same way, the gospel is bearing fruit and growing throughout the whole world— just as it has been doing among you since the day you heard it and truly understood God's grace. You learned it from Epaphras, our dear fellow servant, who is a faithful minister of Christ on our behalf, and who also told us of your love in the Spirit" (NIV).

Observation: Write what stands out to you.

> When you combine faith and love, you get hope. We must remember that our hope is in heaven; it is yet to come. The gospel is the Word of truth. The gospel is continually bearing fruit and growing from the first day to the last. It just takes one person to change a whole community…Epaphras.

Application: Apply this scripture to your own life.

> God used one man, Epaphras, to change a whole town. I was reminded that we are simply called to tell others about Christ; it's God's job to spread the gospel, to grow it, and have it bear fruit. I felt today's verses were almost directly spoken to Love God Greatly women: "The gospel is bearing fruit and growing throughout the whole world—just as it has been doing among you since the day you heard it and truly understood God's grace."

It's so fun when God's Word comes alive and encourages us in our current situation! My passionate desire is that all the women involved in our LGG Bible study will understand God's grace and have a thirst for His Word. I was moved by this quote from my Bible commentary today: "God's Word is not just for our information, it is for our transformation."

Prayer: Pray over this.

> Dear Lord, please help me to be an "Epaphras," to tell others about You and then leave the results in Your loving hands. Please help me to understand and apply personally what I have read today to my life, thereby becoming more and more like You each and every day. Help me to live a life that bears the fruit of faith and love, anchoring my hope in heaven, not here on earth. Help me to remember that the best is yet to come!

SOAP It Up

Remember, the most important ingredients in the SOAP method are your interaction with God's Word and your application of His Word to your life:

> Blessed is the one who does not walk in step with the wicked or stand in the way that sinners take or sit in the company of mockers, but whose delight is in the law of the LORD, and who meditates on his law day and night. That person is like a tree planted by streams of water, which yields its fruit in season and whose leaf does not wither—whatever they do prospers. (Ps. 1:1–3, NIV)

Reading Plan

Week 1 - Peter

MON.	Simon (his character)	READ: John 18:10; 13:5-9	SOAP: John 13:8-9
TUES.	The Calling "Fisher of Men"	READ: Luke 5:1-11	SOAP: Luke 5:10-11
WED.	Peter Walks on Water	READ: Matthew 14:22-33	SOAP: Matthew 14:28-33
THURS.	Peter Denies Jesus	READ: Matthew 26:30-35; 69-75	SOAP: Matthew 26:34-35; 74-75
FRI.	Peter's Faith Makes Him Bold	READ: Matthew 16:13-18; Acts 4:1-13	SOAP: Mt 16:18; Acts 4:13

RESPONSE DAY

Week 2 - John & James

MON.	Called by Jesus	READ: Mark 1:16-20; 3:17	SOAP: Mark 1:20
TUES.	Two Hot Heads	READ: Luke 9:51-56	SOAP: Luke 9:53-55
WED.	The Odd Request	READ: Mark 10:35-45	SOAP: Mark 10:35-38
THURS.	The Beloved Disciple	READ: John 13:23; 19:25-26; 20:2; 21:7	SOAP: John 19:25-26
FRI.	John in Exile & James' Death	READ: Revelation 1:1-11; Acts 12:1-4	SOAP: Rev. 1:9; Acts 12:1-2

RESPONSE DAY

Week 3 - The Unknown Disciples - James, Andrew, Jude (Thaddeus), Bartholomew (Nathanael)

		READ	SOAP
MON.	James, Son of Alphaeus (James the Lesser)	READ: Mt 10:2-4; Mk 15:40	SOAP: Mt 10:2-4; Mk 15:40
TUES.	Thaddeus (Judas)	READ: John 14:15-26	SOAP: John 14:22-23
WED.	Andrew Introduces Peter to Jesus	READ: John 1:35-42	SOAP: John 1:40
THURS.	Bartholomew (Nathanael) the Honest	READ: Jn 1:47; Prov 10:9; 1 Pet 3:10-12	SOAP: Jn 1:47; 1 Pet 3:10-12
FRI.	Not all 12 were well known, but their reward is great	READ: Mt 19:22-30	SOAP: Mt 19:28-30

RESPONSE DAY

Week 4 - Matthew, Simon the Zealot

		READ	SOAP
MON.	Matthew	READ: Matthew 9:9-13	SOAP: Matthew 9:11-13
TUES.	Matthew	READ: 1 John 1:8-9	SOAP: 1 John 1:9
WED.	Resist greed, be generous	READ: Ecclesiastes 5:10; Hebrews 13:5; Prov. 14:21	SOAP: Eccl. 5:10; Prov. 14:21
THURS.	Simon the Zealot	READ: Luke 6:12-15; Romans 12:11	SOAP: Romans 12:11
FRI.	We are made to be zealous	READ: Titus 2:11-14	SOAP: Titus 2:14

RESPONSE DAY

Week 5 - Thomas

MON.	Thomas doubts the risen Lord	READ: John 20:24-29	SOAP: John 20:27-29
TUES.	Thomas doubts Christ's ability to provide	READ: John 14:1-7	SOAP: John 14:5-7
WED.	Everyone struggles with doubt	READ: Psalm 13	SOAP: Psalm 13
THURS.	Danger of Doubt	READ: James 1:5-8	SOAP: James 1:5-8
FRI.	Faith comes and grows through the word	READ: Romans 10:17; Philippians 1:6	SOAP: Rom. 10:17; Phil. 1:6

RESPONSE DAY

Week 6 - Philip & Judas Iscariot

MON.	Philip	READ: John 6:1-14	SOAP: John 6:5-7
TUES.	God Provides	READ: Philippians 4:19; Matthew 19:26	SOAP: Phil. 4:19; Matthew 19:26
WED.	Jesus is God	READ: John 14:8-9; 10:30	SOAP: John 14:8-9; 10:30
THURS.	Judas Iscariot	READ: John 13:21-30; Matthew 16:14-16; 27:5-7	SOAP: Matthew 16:14-16
FRI.	God Saves the Repentant	READ: Romans 3:23; 5:8; 10:9	SOAP: Romans 3:23; 5:8; 10:9

RESPONSE DAY

Goals

WE BELIEVE it's important to write out goals for this study. Take some time now and write three goals you would like to focus on as you begin to rise each day and dig into God's Word. Make sure and refer back to these goals throughout the next six weeks to help you stay focused. You can do it!

My goals are:

1.

2.

3.

Signature: _____

Date: _____

Introduction

MANY CAN NAME the cast of their favorite TV show or the full roster of their favorite team. But few Christians know the names of all twelve of Jesus's disciples. *These are the twelve: Simon, who is called Peter, and Andrew his brother; James the son of Zebedee, and John his brother; Philip and Bartholomew; Thomas, and Matthew the tax collector; James the son of Alphaeus, and Thaddaeus; Simon the Zealot, and Judas Iscariot, who betrayed him (Matthew 10:2-4).*

These were the twelve men Jesus chose to become his closest companions and ministers during his three-year ministry. And these are the twelve men whose lives we will be studying throughout the next six weeks.

As we learn from the twelve disciples, it is important to recognize what a disciple actually is. Generally, a disciple is someone who follows the teaching and example of their mentor. **But the disciples of Jesus are more than mere devotees.** These twelve were called to leave family, friends, job, home, and comfort in order to become His students. Jesus's disciples listened to Him, believed in Him, and followed His example, even to the point of giving their lives for the sake of proclaiming the good news of Jesus Christ. **A true disciple sees Jesus not only as a mentor, but as the Messiah; more than a spiritual guru, but as the Son of God.**

As we look at the twelve, we need to understand who they really were. Many of us are tempted to view certain biblical characters as super spiritual. Men like Abraham, Moses, Joseph, and David look to have faith beyond anything that of normal people. While the twelve disciples may have had a rocky start, all but one seem to end up with faith that moved mountains. But we need to remember that all of the people in Scripture - including the twelve disciples - were ordinary men. They were people who, like you and me, were far from perfect. They struggled with faith, understanding, selfishness, rashness, misplaced zeal, and fear. They sinned and were sinned against and desperately needed the blood sacrifice of the One they followed.

In this study we will look at all twelve of these men; flaws and all. What is interesting is that while we may know a lot about some like Peter and John, we know next to nothing about others like Bartholomew and Thaddeus. When it comes to some of these lesser known disciples, we will take a look at the character traits that they have come to be known for.

As it became clear to the disciples who Jesus really was, and as the Holy Spirit came upon them, their faith grew and their passion for their Savior was ignited. They became men who were not only willing to give up family and home, but men who were willing to give up their very lives for the glory of Jesus.

This did not happen because they were more special than any of us. **This is the result of the power of God in them.** Men who were fearful became bold. Men who were ignorant became wise. Men who were confused as to where they were to go or what they were to do became clear about their calling.

A real encounter with Jesus changes people.

He gives new life and new meaning to life. He gives passion and a clear direction for where our life is headed. He gives value to what we do and wisdom for the decisions that we need to make.

As you study these twelve men, look not only at the various experiences these men had and how this close encounter with Jesus changed them, but how you can be changed as well.

Week 1

Week 1 Challenge (Note: You can find this listed in our Monday blog post):

Prayer focus for this week: Spend time praying for your family members.

	Praying	Praise
Monday		
Tuesday		
Wednesday		
Thursday		
Friday		

And when they had
brought their boats to land,
they left everything and followed him.

LUKE 5:11

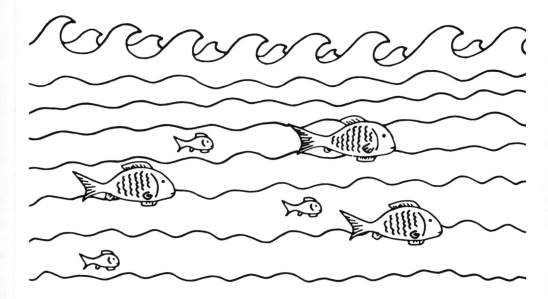

Scripture for Week 1

MONDAY

JOHN 18:10

[10] Then Simon Peter, having a sword, drew it and struck the high priest's servant and cut off his right ear. (The servant's name was Malchus.)

JOHN 13:5-9

[5] Then he poured water into a basin and began to wash the disciples' feet and to wipe them with the towel that was wrapped around him. [6] He came to Simon Peter, who said to him, "Lord, do you wash my feet?" [7] Jesus answered him, "What I am doing you do not understand now, but afterward you will understand."[8] Peter said to him, "You shall never wash my feet." Jesus answered him, "If I do not wash you, you have no share with me." [9] Simon Peter said to him, "Lord, not my feet only but also my hands and my head!"

TUESDAY

LUKE 5:1-11

[1] On one occasion, while the crowd was pressing in on him to hear the word of God, he was standing by the lake of Gennesaret, [2] and he saw two boats by the lake, but the fishermen had gone out of them and were washing their nets.[3] Getting into one of the boats, which was Simon's, he asked him to put out a little from the land. And he sat down and taught the people from the boat. [4] And when he had finished speaking, he said to Simon, "Put out into the deep and let down your nets for a catch." [5] And Simon answered, "Master, we toiled all night and took nothing! But at your word I will let down the nets." [6] And when they had done this, they enclosed a large number of fish, and their nets were breaking. [7] They signaled to their partners in the other boat to come and help them. And they came and filled both the boats, so that they began to sink. [8] But when Simon Peter saw it, he fell down at Jesus' knees, saying, "Depart from me, for I am a sinful man, O Lord."[9] For he

and all who were with him were astonished at the catch of fish that they had taken, [10] and so also were James and John, sons of Zebedee, who were partners with Simon. And Jesus said to Simon, "Do not be afraid; from now on you will be catching men." [11] And when they had brought their boats to land, they left everything and followed him.

WEDNESDAY

MATTHEW 14:22-33

[22] Immediately he made the disciples get into the boat and go before him to the other side, while he dismissed the crowds. [23] And after he had dismissed the crowds, he went up on the mountain by himself to pray. When evening came, he was there alone, [24] but the boat by this time was a long way from the land, beaten by the waves, for the wind was against them. [25] And in the fourth watch of the night he came to them, walking on the sea. [26] But when the disciples saw him walking on the sea, they were terrified, and said, "It is a ghost!" and they cried out in fear. [27] But immediately Jesus spoke to them, saying, "Take heart; it is I. Do not be afraid."

[28] And Peter answered him, "Lord, if it is you, command me to come to you on the water." [29] He said, "Come." So Peter got out of the boat and walked on the water and came to Jesus. [30] But when he saw the wind, he was afraid, and beginning to sink he cried out, "Lord, save me." [31] Jesus immediately reached out his hand and took hold of him, saying to him, "O you of little faith, why did you doubt?"[32] And when they got into the boat, the wind ceased. [33] And those in the boat worshiped him, saying, "Truly you are the Son of God."

THURSDAY

MATTHEW 26:30-35

[30] And when they had sung a hymn, they went out to the Mount of Olives. [31] Then Jesus said to them, "You will all fall away because of me this night. For it is written, 'I will strike the shepherd, and the

sheep of the flock will be scattered.' 32 But after I am raised up, I will go before you to Galilee." 33 Peter answered him, "Though they all fall away because of you, I will never fall away." 34 Jesus said to him, "Truly, I tell you, this very night, before the rooster crows, you will deny me three times."35 Peter said to him, "Even if I must die with you, I will not deny you!" And all the disciples said the same.

MATTHEW 26:69-75

69 Now Peter was sitting outside in the courtyard. And a servant girl came up to him and said, "You also were with Jesus the Galilean." 70 But he denied it before them all, saying, "I do not know what you mean." 71 And when he went out to the entrance, another servant girl saw him, and she said to the bystanders, "This man was with Jesus of Nazareth." 72 And again he denied it with an oath: "I do not know the man." 73 After a little while the bystanders came up and said to Peter, "Certainly you too are one of them, for your accent betrays you." 74 Then he began to invoke a curse on himself and to swear, "I do not know the man." And immediately the rooster crowed. 75 And Peter remembered the saying of Jesus, "Before the rooster crows, you will deny me three times." And he went out and wept bitterly.

FRIDAY

MATTHEW 16:13-18

13 Now when Jesus came into the district of Caesarea Philippi, he asked his disciples, "Who do people say that the Son of Man is?" 14 And they said, "Some say John the Baptist, others say Elijah, and others Jeremiah or one of the prophets." 15 He said to them, "But who do you say that I am?" 16 Simon Peter replied, "You are the Christ, the Son of the living God." 17 And Jesus answered him, "Blessed are you, Simon Bar-Jonah! For flesh and blood has not revealed this to you, but my Father who is in heaven. 18 And I tell you, you are Peter, and on this rock I will build my church, and the gates of hell shall not prevail against it.

ACTS 4:1-13

[1] And as they were speaking to the people, the priests and the captain of the temple and the Sadducees came upon them, [2] greatly annoyed because they were teaching the people and proclaiming in Jesus the resurrection from the dead. [3] And they arrested them and put them in custody until the next day, for it was already evening. [4] But many of those who had heard the word believed, and the number of the men came to about five thousand.

[5] On the next day their rulers and elders and scribes gathered together in Jerusalem, [6] with Annas the high priest and Caiaphas and John and Alexander, and all who were of the high-priestly family. [7] And when they had set them in the midst, they inquired, "By what power or by what name did you do this?" [8] Then Peter, filled with the Holy Spirit, said to them, "Rulers of the people and elders, [9] if we are being examined today concerning a good deed done to a crippled man, by what means this man has been healed, [10] let it be known to all of you and to all the people of Israel that by the name of Jesus Christ of Nazareth, whom you crucified, whom God raised from the dead—by him this man is standing before you well. [11] This Jesus is the stone that was rejected by you, the builders, which has become the cornerstone. [12] And there is salvation in no one else, for there is no other name under heaven given among men by which we must be saved."

[13] Now when they saw the boldness of Peter and John, and perceived that they were uneducated, common men, they were astonished. And they recognized that they had been with Jesus.

Monday

READ: John 18:10; 13:5-9
SOAP: John 13:8-9

Scripture - Write out the **Scripture** passage for the day.

Observations - Write down 1 or 2 **observations** from the passage.

Monday

Applications - Write down 1 or 2 **applications** from the passage.

Pray - Write out a **prayer** over what you learned from today's passage.

-Visit our website today for the corresponding blog post!-

READ: Luke 5:1-11
SOAP: Luke 5:10-11

Scripture - Write out the **Scripture** passage for the day.

Observations - Write down 1 or 2 **observations** from the passage.

Tuesday

Applications - Write down 1 or 2 **applications** from the passage.

Pray - Write out a **prayer** over what you learned from today's passage.

Wednesday

READ: Matthew 14:22-33
SOAP: Matthew 14:28-33

Scripture - Write out the **Scripture** passage for the day.

Observations - Write down 1 or 2 **observations** from the passage.

Wednesday

Applications - Write down 1 or 2 **applications** from the passage.

Pray - Write out a **prayer** over what you learned from today's passage.

-Visit our website today for the corresponding blog post!-

Thursday

READ: Matthew 26:30-35; 69-75
SOAP: Matthew 26:34-35; 74-75

Scripture - Write out the **Scripture** passage for the day.

Observations - Write down 1 or 2 **observations** from the passage.

Thursday

Applications - Write down 1 or 2 **applications** from the passage.

Pray - Write out a **prayer** over what you learned from today's passage.

Friday

READ: Matthew 16:13-18; Acts 4:1-13

SOAP: Matthew 16:18; Acts 4:13

Scripture - Write out the **Scripture** passage for the day.

Observations - Write down 1 or 2 **observations** from the passage.

Friday

Applications - Write down 1 or 2 **applications** from the passage.

Pray - Write out a **prayer** over what you learned from today's passage.

-Visit our website today for the corresponding blog post!-

Reflection Questions

1. What character traits do you see in Peter?

2. What does it mean to be "fishers of men"?

3. What lessons do we learn about faith when we read the story about Peter walking on water?

4. Why did Peter deny Jesus? How do we deny Jesus?

5. How did mature faith change Peter?

My Response

Week 2

Week 2 Challenge (Note: You can find this listed in our Monday blog post):

Prayer focus for this week: Spend time praying for your country.

	Praying	Praise
Monday		
Tuesday		
Wednesday		
Thursday		
Friday		

For even the Son of Man came
not to be served but to serve,
and to give his life
as a ransom for many.

MARK 10:45

Scripture for Week 2

MONDAY

MARK 1:16-20

[16] Passing alongside the Sea of Galilee, he saw Simon and Andrew the brother of Simon casting a net into the sea, for they were fishermen. [17] And Jesus said to them, "Follow me, and I will make you become fishers of men." [18] And immediately they left their nets and followed him. [19] And going on a little farther, he saw James the son of Zebedee and John his brother, who were in their boat mending the nets. [20] And immediately he called them, and they left their father Zebedee in the boat with the hired servants and followed him.

MARK 3:17

[17] James the son of Zebedee and John the brother of James (to whom he gave the name Boanerges, that is, Sons of Thunder);

TUESDAY

LUKE 9:51-56

[51] When the days drew near for him to be taken up, he set his face to go to Jerusalem. [52] And he sent messengers ahead of him, who went and entered a village of the Samaritans, to make preparations for him. [53] But the people did not receive him, because his face was set toward Jerusalem. [54] And when his disciples James and John saw it, they said, "Lord, do you want us to tell fire to come down from heaven and consume them?" [55] But he turned and rebuked them. [56] And they went on to another village.

WEDNESDAY

MARK 10:35-45

[35] And James and John, the sons of Zebedee, came up to him and said to him, "Teacher, we want you to do for us whatever we ask

of you." ³⁶ And he said to them, "What do you want me to do for you?" ³⁷ And they said to him, "Grant us to sit, one at your right hand and one at your left, in your glory." ³⁸ Jesus said to them, "You do not know what you are asking. Are you able to drink the cup that I drink, or to be baptized with the baptism with which I am baptized?" ³⁹ And they said to him, "We are able." And Jesus said to them, "The cup that I drink you will drink, and with the baptism with which I am baptized, you will be baptized, ⁴⁰ but to sit at my right hand or at my left is not mine to grant, but it is for those for whom it has been prepared." ⁴¹ And when the ten heard it, they began to be indignant at James and John. ⁴² And Jesus called them to him and said to them, "You know that those who are considered rulers of the Gentiles lord it over them, and their great ones exercise authority over them. ⁴³ But it shall not be so among you. But whoever would be great among you must be your servant, ⁴⁴ and whoever would be first among you must be slave of all. ⁴⁵ For even the Son of Man came not to be served but to serve, and to give his life as a ransom for many."

THURSDAY

JOHN 13:23

²³ One of his disciples, whom Jesus loved, was reclining at table at Jesus' side

JOHN 19:25-26

²⁵ but standing by the cross of Jesus were his mother and his mother's sister, Mary the wife of Clopas, and Mary Magdalene. ²⁶ When Jesus saw his mother and the disciple whom he loved standing nearby, he said to his mother, "Woman, behold, your son!"

JOHN 20:2

² So she ran and went to Simon Peter and the other disciple, the one whom Jesus loved, and said to them, "They have taken the Lord out of the tomb, and we do not know where they have laid him."

JOHN 21:7

[7] That disciple whom Jesus loved therefore said to Peter, "It is the Lord!" When Simon Peter heard that it was the Lord, he put on his outer garment, for he was stripped for work, and threw himself into the sea.

FRIDAY

REVELATION 1:1-11

[1] The revelation of Jesus Christ, which God gave him to show to his servants the things that must soon take place. He made it known by sending his angel to his servant John, [2] who bore witness to the word of God and to the testimony of Jesus Christ, even to all that he saw. [3] Blessed is the one who reads aloud the words of this prophecy, and blessed are those who hear, and who keep what is written in it, for the time is near.

[4] John to the seven churches that are in Asia:

Grace to you and peace from him who is and who was and who is to come, and from the seven spirits who are before his throne, [5] and from Jesus Christ the faithful witness, the firstborn of the dead, and the ruler of kings on earth.

To him who loves us and has freed us from our sins by his blood [6] and made us a kingdom, priests to his God and Father, to him be glory and dominion forever and ever. Amen. [7] Behold, he is coming with the clouds, and every eye will see him, even those who pierced him, and all tribes of the earth will wail on account of him. Even so. Amen.

[8] "I am the Alpha and the Omega," says the Lord God, "who is and who was and who is to come, the Almighty."

[9] I, John, your brother and partner in the tribulation and the kingdom and the patient endurance that are in Jesus, was on the island called Patmos on account of the word of God and the testimony of Jesus. [10] I was in the Spirit on the Lord's day, and I heard behind me a loud voice like a trumpet [11] saying, "Write what you see in a book and send it to the seven churches, to Ephesus and

to Smyrna and to Pergamum and to Thyatira and to Sardis and to Philadelphia and to Laodicea."

ACTS 12:1-4

[1] About that time Herod the king laid violent hands on some who belonged to the church. [2] He killed James the brother of John with the sword, [3] and when he saw that it pleased the Jews, he proceeded to arrest Peter also. This was during the days of Unleavened Bread. [4] And when he had seized him, he put him in prison, delivering him over to four squads of soldiers to guard him, intending after the Passover to bring him out to the people.

Monday

READ: Mark 1:16-20; 3:17
SOAP: Mark 1:20

Scripture - Write out the **Scripture** passage for the day.

Observations - Write down 1 or 2 **observations** from the passage.

Monday

Applications - Write down 1 or 2 **applications** from the passage.

Pray - Write out a **prayer** over what you learned from today's passage.

-Visit our website today for the corresponding blog post!-

Tuesday

READ: Luke 9:51-56

SOAP: Luke 9:53-55

Scripture - Write out the **Scripture** passage for the day.

Observations - Write down 1 or 2 **observations** from the passage.

Tuesday

Applications - Write down 1 or 2 **applications** from the passage.

Pray - Write out a **prayer** over what you learned from today's passage.

Wednesday

READ: Mark 10:35-45

SOAP: Mark 10:35-38

Scripture - Write out the **Scripture** passage for the day.

Observations - Write down 1 or 2 **observations** from the passage.

Wednesday

Applications - Write down 1 or 2 **applications** from the passage.

Pray - Write out a **prayer** over what you learned from today's passage.

-Visit our website today for the corresponding blog post!-

Thursday

READ: John 13:23; 19:25-26; 20:2; 21:7
SOAP: John 19:25-26

Scripture - Write out the **Scripture** passage for the day.

Observations - Write down 1 or 2 **observations** from the passage.

Thursday

Applications - Write down 1 or 2 **applications** from the passage.

Pray - Write out a **prayer** over what you learned from today's passage.

Friday

READ: Revelation 1:1-11; Acts 12:1-4
SOAP: Revelation 1:9; Acts 12:1-2

Scripture - Write out the **Scripture** passage for the day.

Observations - Write down 1 or 2 **observations** from the passage.

Friday

Applications - Write down 1 or 2 **applications** from the passage.

Pray - Write out a **prayer** over what you learned from today's passage.

-Visit our website today for the corresponding blog post!-

Reflection Questions

1. Did James and John hesitate to follow Jesus? In what ways have you followed Jesus without hesitation? In what ways have you hesitated?

2. James and John were called "sons of thunder". What does this tell us about their character?

3. What request did the two brothers have of Jesus? Was this a step of faith or foolishness?

4. A number of times John is called "the one whom Jesus loved". What does this tell us about their friendship? What does this tell us about Jesus?

5. How did James and John die?

My Response

Week 3

Week 3 Challenge (Note: You can find this listed in our Monday blog post):

Prayer focus for this week: Spend time praying for your friends.

	Praying	Praise
Monday		
Tuesday		
Wednesday		
Thursday		
Friday		

And everyone who has left houses or brothers or sisters or father or mother or children or lands, for my name's sake, will receive a hundredfold and will inherit eternal life.

MATTHEW 19:29

Scripture for Week 3

MONDAY

MATTHEW 10:2-4

[2] The names of the twelve apostles are these: first, Simon, who is called Peter, and Andrew his brother; James the son of Zebedee, and John his brother; [3] Philip and Bartholomew; Thomas and Matthew the tax collector; James the son of Alphaeus, and Thaddaeus; [4] Simon the Zealot, and Judas Iscariot, who betrayed him.

MARK 15:40

[40] There were also women looking on from a distance, among whom were Mary Magdalene, and Mary the mother of James the younger and of Joses, and Salome.

TUESDAY

JOHN 14:15-26

[15] "If you love me, you will keep my commandments. [16] And I will ask the Father, and he will give you another Helper, to be with you forever, [17] even the Spirit of truth, whom the world cannot receive, because it neither sees him nor knows him. You know him, for he dwells with you and will be in you.

[18] "I will not leave you as orphans; I will come to you. [19] Yet a little while and the world will see me no more, but you will see me. Because I live, you also will live. [20] In that day you will know that I am in my Father, and you in me, and I in you. [21] Whoever has my commandments and keeps them, he it is who loves me. And he who loves me will be loved by my Father, and I will love him and manifest myself to him." [22] Judas (not Iscariot) said to him, "Lord, how is it that you will manifest yourself to us, and not to the world?" [23] Jesus answered him, "If anyone loves me, he will keep my word, and my Father will love him, and we will come to him and make our home with him. [24] Whoever does not love me does not keep my words. And the word that you hear is not mine but the Father's who sent me.

²⁵ "These things I have spoken to you while I am still with you. ²⁶ But the Helper, the Holy Spirit, whom the Father will send in my name, he will teach you all things and bring to your remembrance all that I have said to you.

WEDNESDAY

JOHN 1:35-42

³⁵ The next day again John was standing with two of his disciples, ³⁶ and he looked at Jesus as he walked by and said, "Behold, the Lamb of God!" ³⁷ The two disciples heard him say this, and they followed Jesus. ³⁸ Jesus turned and saw them following and said to them, "What are you seeking?" And they said to him, "Rabbi" (which means Teacher), "where are you staying?" ³⁹ He said to them, "Come and you will see." So they came and saw where he was staying, and they stayed with him that day, for it was about the tenth hour. ⁴⁰ One of the two who heard John speak and followed Jesus was Andrew, Simon Peter's brother. ⁴¹ He first found his own brother Simon and said to him, "We have found the Messiah" (which means Christ). ⁴² He brought him to Jesus. Jesus looked at him and said, "You are Simon the son of John. You shall be called Cephas" (which means Peter).

THURSDAY

JOHN 1:47

⁴⁷ Jesus saw Nathanael coming toward him and said of him, "Behold, an Israelite indeed, in whom there is no deceit!"

PROVERBS 10:9

⁹ Whoever walks in integrity walks securely,
  but he who makes his ways crooked will be found out.

1 PETER 3:10-12

¹⁰ For

"Whoever desires to love life
  and see good days,
let him keep his tongue from evil
  and his lips from speaking deceit;
¹¹ let him turn away from evil and do good;
  let him seek peace and pursue it.
¹² For the eyes of the Lord are on the righteous,
  and his ears are open to their prayer.
But the face of the Lord is against those who do evil."

FRIDAY

MATTHEW 19:22-30

²² When the young man heard this he went away sorrowful, for he had great possessions.

²³ And Jesus said to his disciples, "Truly, I say to you, only with difficulty will a rich person enter the kingdom of heaven. ²⁴ Again I tell you, it is easier for a camel to go through the eye of a needle than for a rich person to enter the kingdom of God." ²⁵ When the disciples heard this, they were greatly astonished, saying, "Who then can be saved?" ²⁶ But Jesus looked at them and said, "With man this is impossible, but with God all things are possible." ²⁷ Then Peter said in reply, "See, we have left everything and followed you. What then will we have?" ²⁸ Jesus said to them, "Truly, I say to you, in the new world, when the Son of Man will sit on his glorious throne, you who have followed me will also sit on twelve thrones, judging the twelve tribes of Israel. ²⁹ And everyone who has left houses or brothers or sisters or father or mother or children or lands, for my name's sake, will receive a hundredfold and will inherit eternal life. ³⁰ But many who are first will be last, and the last first.

Monday

READ: Matthew 10:2-4; Mark 15:40
SOAP: Matthew 10:2-4; Mark 15:40

Scripture - Write out the **Scripture** passage for the day.

Observations - Write down 1 or 2 **observations** from the passage.

Monday

Applications - Write down 1 or 2 **applications** from the passage.

Pray - Write out a **prayer** over what you learned from today's passage.

-Visit our website today for the corresponding blog post!-

Tuesday

READ: John 14:15-26
SOAP: John 14:22-23

Scripture - Write out the **Scripture** passage for the day.

Observations - Write down 1 or 2 **observations** from the passage.

Tuesday

Applications - Write down 1 or 2 **applications** from the passage.

Pray - Write out a **prayer** over what you learned from today's passage.

Wednesday

READ: John 1:35-42

SOAP: John 1:40

Scripture - Write out the **Scripture** passage for the day.

Observations - Write down 1 or 2 **observations** from the passage.

Wednesday

Applications - Write down 1 or 2 **applications** from the passage.

Pray - Write out a **prayer** over what you learned from today's passage.

-Visit our website today for the corresponding blog post!-

Thursday

READ: John 1:47; Proverbs 10:9; 1 Peter 3:10-12

SOAP: John 1:47; 1 Peter 3:10-12

Scripture - Write out the **Scripture** passage for the day.

Observations - Write down 1 or 2 **observations** from the passage.

Thursday

Applications - Write down 1 or 2 **applications** from the passage.

Pray - Write out a **prayer** over what you learned from today's passage.

Friday

READ: Matthew 19:22-30

SOAP: Matthew 19:28-30

Scripture - Write out the **Scripture** passage for the day.

Observations - Write down 1 or 2 **observations** from the passage.

Friday

Applications - Write down 1 or 2 **applications** from the passage.

Pray - Write out a **prayer** over what you learned from today's passage.

-Visit our website today for the corresponding blog post!-

Reflection Questions

1. Why do you think little is told to us about some of the disciples?

2. What question did Judas ask Jesus and how was it answered?

3. Why do you think Andrew introduced Peter to Jesus? What important fact did Andrew understand about Jesus?

4. Of all the things we could have been told about Nathanael (Bartholomew), we are told that "there was no deceit in him". What does this tell us about the importance of honesty? Would this be said of you? What does this mean when it comes to training our children or how we handle dishonesty?

5. The disciples left everything to follow Jesus. While some are now considered "famous" and others are not, their reward is the same. What did Jesus say will await them?

My Response

Week 4

Week 4 Challenge (Note: You can find this listed in our Monday blog post):

Prayer focus for this week: Spend time praying for your church.

	Praying	Praise
Monday		
Tuesday		
Wednesday		
Thursday		
Friday		

Whoever despises his
neighbor is a sinner,
but blessed is he who
is generous to the poor.

PROVERBS 14:21

MONDAY

MATTHEW 9:9-13

⁹ As Jesus passed on from there, he saw a man called Matthew sitting at the tax booth, and he said to him, "Follow me." And he rose and followed him.

¹⁰ And as Jesus reclined at table in the house, behold, many tax collectors and sinners came and were reclining with Jesus and his disciples. ¹¹ And when the Pharisees saw this, they said to his disciples, "Why does your teacher eat with tax collectors and sinners?" ¹² But when he heard it, he said, "Those who are well have no need of a physician, but those who are sick. ¹³ Go and learn what this means: 'I desire mercy, and not sacrifice.' For I came not to call the righteous, but sinners."

TUESDAY

1 JOHN 1:8-9

⁸ If we say we have no sin, we deceive ourselves, and the truth is not in us. ⁹ If we confess our sins, he is faithful and just to forgive us our sins and to cleanse us from all unrighteousness.

WEDNESDAY

ECCLESIASTES 5:10

¹⁰ He who loves money will not be satisfied with money, nor he who loves wealth with his income; this also is vanity.

HEBREWS 13:5

⁵ Keep your life free from love of money, and be content with what you have, for he has said, "I will never leave you nor forsake you."

PROVERBS 14:21

21Whoever despises his neighbor is a sinner,
  but blessed is he who is generous to the poor.

THURSDAY

LUKE 6:12-15

12 In these days he went out to the mountain to pray, and
all night he continued in prayer to God. 13 And when day
came, he called his disciples and chose from them twelve,
whom he named apostles: 14 Simon, whom he named Peter,
and Andrew his brother, and James and John, and Philip, and
Bartholomew, 15 and Matthew, and Thomas, and James the son of
Alphaeus, and Simon who was called the Zealot,

ROMANS 12:11

11 Do not be slothful in zeal, be fervent in spirit, serve the Lord.

FRIDAY

TITUS 2:11-14

11 For the grace of God has appeared, bringing salvation for all
people, 12 training us to renounce ungodliness and worldly passions,
and to live self-controlled, upright, and godly lives in the present
age, 13 waiting for our blessed hope, the appearing of the glory of
our great God and Savior Jesus Christ, 14 who gave himself for us
to redeem us from all lawlessness and to purify for himself a people
for his own possession who are zealous for good works.

READ: Matthew 9:9-13
SOAP: Matthew 9:11-13

Scripture - Write out the **Scripture** passage for the day.

Observations - Write down 1 or 2 **observations** from the passage.

Monday

Applications - Write down 1 or 2 **applications** from the passage.

Pray - Write out a **prayer** over what you learned from today's passage.

-Visit our website today for the corresponding blog post!-

Tuesday

READ: 1 John 1:8-9
SOAP: 1 John 1:9

Scripture - Write out the **Scripture** passage for the day.

Observations - Write down 1 or 2 **observations** from the passage.

Tuesday

Applications - Write down 1 or 2 **applications** from the passage.

Pray - Write out a **prayer** over what you learned from today's passage.

Wednesday

READ: Ecclesiastes 5:10; Hebrews 13:5; Proverbs 14:21
SOAP: Eccl. 5:10; Proverbs 14:21

Scripture - Write out the **Scripture** passage for the day.

Observations - Write down 1 or 2 **observations** from the passage.

Wednesday

Applications - Write down 1 or 2 **applications** from the passage.

Pray - Write out a **prayer** over what you learned from today's passage.

-Visit our website today for the corresponding blog post!-

Thursday

READ: Luke 6:12-15; Romans 12:11

SOAP: Romans 12:11

Scripture - Write out the **Scripture** passage for the day.

Observations - Write down 1 or 2 **observations** from the passage.

Thursday

Applications - Write down 1 or 2 **applications** from the passage.

Pray - Write out a **prayer** over what you learned from today's passage.

Friday

READ: Titus 2:11-14
SOAP: Titus 2:14

Scripture - Write out the **Scripture** passage for the day.

Observations - Write down 1 or 2 **observations** from the passage.

Friday

Applications - Write down 1 or 2 **applications** from the passage.

Pray - Write out a **prayer** over what you learned from today's passage.

-Visit our website today for the corresponding blog post!-

Reflection Questions

1. What was Matthew's job and why was it such a scandal for Jesus to interact with him? How did Jesus respond to the criticism?

2. No matter how bad our sins are, what is promised if we confess our sins?

3. As a tax collector Matthew would have been thought of as greedy. Why is greed a sin? In what ways do you struggle with greed?

4. Simon was known as a Zealot. What does this mean and what does this tell us about his personality?

5. We are created to be zealous. What should that look like in our lives?

My Response

Week 5

Week 5 Challenge (Note: You can find this listed in our Monday blog post):

Prayer focus for this week: Spend time praying for your church.

	Praying	Praise
Monday		
Tuesday		
Wednesday		
Thursday		
Friday		

MONDAY

JOHN 20:24-29

24 Now Thomas, one of the twelve, called the Twin, was not with them when Jesus came. 25 So the other disciples told him, "We have seen the Lord." But he said to them, "Unless I see in his hands the mark of the nails, and place my finger into the mark of the nails, and place my hand into his side, I will never believe."

26 Eight days later, his disciples were inside again, and Thomas was with them. Although the doors were locked, Jesus came and stood among them and said, "Peace be with you." 27 Then he said to Thomas, "Put your finger here, and see my hands; and put out your hand, and place it in my side. Do not disbelieve, but believe." 28 Thomas answered him, "My Lord and my God!" 29 Jesus said to him, "Have you believed because you have seen me? Blessed are those who have not seen and yet have believed."

TUESDAY

JOHN 14:1-7

1 "Let not your hearts be troubled. Believe in God; believe also in me. 2 In my Father's house are many rooms. If it were not so, would I have told you that I go to prepare a place for you? 3 And if I go and prepare a place for you, I will come again and will take you to myself, that where I am you may be also. 4 And you know the way to where I am going." 5 Thomas said to him, "Lord, we do not know where you are going. How can we know the way?" 6 Jesus said to him, "I am the way, and the truth, and the life. No one comes to the Father except through me. 7 If you had known me, you would have known my Father also. From now on you do know him and have seen him."

WEDNESDAY

PSALM 13

1 How long, O Lord? Will you forget me forever?
 How long will you hide your face from me?
2 How long must I take counsel in my soul
 and have sorrow in my heart all the day?
How long shall my enemy be exalted over me?
3 Consider and answer me, O Lord my God;
 light up my eyes, lest I sleep the sleep of death,
4 lest my enemy say, "I have prevailed over him,"
 lest my foes rejoice because I am shaken.
5 But I have trusted in your steadfast love;
 my heart shall rejoice in your salvation.
6 I will sing to the Lord,
 because he has dealt bountifully with me.

THURSDAY

JAMES 1:5-8

5 If any of you lacks wisdom, let him ask God, who gives generously to all without reproach, and it will be given him. 6 But let him ask in faith, with no doubting, for the one who doubts is like a wave of the sea that is driven and tossed by the wind. 7 For that person must not suppose that he will receive anything from the Lord; 8 he is a double-minded man, unstable in all his ways.

FRIDAY

ROMANS 10:17

17 So faith comes from hearing, and hearing through the word of Christ.

PHILIPPIANS 1:6

6 And I am sure of this, that he who began a good work in you will bring it to completion at the day of Jesus Christ.

Monday

READ: John 20:24-29
SOAP: John 20:27-29

Scripture - Write out the **Scripture** passage for the day.

Observations - Write down 1 or 2 **observations** from the passage.

Monday

Applications - Write down 1 or 2 **applications** from the passage.

Pray - Write out a **prayer** over what you learned from today's passage.

-Visit our website today for the corresponding blog post!-

READ: John 14:1-7

SOAP: John 14:5-7

Scripture - Write out the **Scripture** passage for the day.

Observations - Write down 1 or 2 **observations** from the passage.

Tuesday

Applications - Write down 1 or 2 **applications** from the passage.

Pray - Write out a **prayer** over what you learned from today's passage.

Wednesday

READ: Psalm 13
SOAP: Psalm 13

Scripture - Write out the **Scripture** passage for the day.

Observations - Write down 1 or 2 **observations** from the passage.

Wednesday

Applications - Write down 1 or 2 **applications** from the passage.

Pray - Write out a **prayer** over what you learned from today's passage.

-Visit our website today for the corresponding blog post!-

Thursday

READ: James 1:5-8
SOAP: James 1:5-8

Scripture - Write out the **Scripture** passage for the day.

Observations - Write down 1 or 2 **observations** from the passage.

Thursday

Applications - Write down 1 or 2 **applications** from the passage.

Pray - Write out a **prayer** over what you learned from today's passage.

Friday

READ: Romans 10:17; Philippians 1:6
SOAP: Romans 10:17; Phil. 1:6

Scripture - Write out the **Scripture** passage for the day.

Observations - Write down 1 or 2 **observations** from the passage.

Friday

Applications - Write down 1 or 2 **applications** from the passage.

Pray - Write out a **prayer** over what you learned from today's passage.

-Visit our website today for the corresponding blog post!-

Reflection Questions

1. Thomas seemed to be quite the skeptic. What proof did he need to believe that Jesus had risen?

2. Thomas struggled to believe that Jesus was going to provide direction for them once he left them. How do we struggle with believing that God will provide for us?

3. In what ways do you struggle with doubt?

4. Why is doubting God dangerous?

5. How is our faith strengthened?

My Response

Week 6

Week 6 Challenge (Note: You can find this listed in our Monday blog post):

Prayer focus for this week: Spend time praying for your church.

	Praying	Praise
Monday		
Tuesday		
Wednesday		
Thursday		
Friday		

but God shows his love for us
in that while we were still sinners,
Christ died for us.

ROMANS 5:8

Scripture for Week 6

MONDAY

JOHN 6:1-14

¹ After this Jesus went away to the other side of the Sea of Galilee, which is the Sea of Tiberias. ² And a large crowd was following him, because they saw the signs that he was doing on the sick. ³ Jesus went up on the mountain, and there he sat down with his disciples. ⁴ Now the Passover, the feast of the Jews, was at hand. ⁵ Lifting up his eyes, then, and seeing that a large crowd was coming toward him, Jesus said to Philip, "Where are we to buy bread, so that these people may eat?" ⁶ He said this to test him, for he himself knew what he would do. ⁷ Philip answered him, "Two hundred denarii worth of bread would not be enough for each of them to get a little." ⁸ One of his disciples, Andrew, Simon Peter's brother, said to him, ⁹ "There is a boy here who has five barley loaves and two fish, but what are they for so many?" ¹⁰ Jesus said, "Have the people sit down." Now there was much grass in the place. So the men sat down, about five thousand in number. ¹¹ Jesus then took the loaves, and when he had given thanks, he distributed them to those who were seated. So also the fish, as much as they wanted. ¹² And when they had eaten their fill, he told his disciples, "Gather up the leftover fragments, that nothing may be lost." ¹³ So they gathered them up and filled twelve baskets with fragments from the five barley loaves left by those who had eaten. ¹⁴ When the people saw the sign that he had done, they said, "This is indeed the Prophet who is to come into the world!"

TUESDAY

PHILIPPIANS 4:19

¹⁹ And my God will supply every need of yours according to his riches in glory in Christ Jesus.

MATTHEW 19:26

²⁶ But Jesus looked at them and said, "With man this is impossible, but with God all things are possible."

WEDNESDAY

JOHN 14:8-9

⁸ Philip said to him, "Lord, show us the Father, and it is enough for us." ⁹ Jesus said to him, "Have I been with you so long, and you still do not know me, Philip? Whoever has seen me has seen the Father. How can you say, 'Show us the Father'?

JOHN 10:30

³⁰ I and the Father are one.

THURSDAY

JOHN 13:21-30

²¹ After saying these things, Jesus was troubled in his spirit, and testified, "Truly, truly, I say to you, one of you will betray me." ²² The disciples looked at one another, uncertain of whom he spoke. ²³ One of his disciples, whom Jesus loved, was reclining at table at Jesus' side, ²⁴ so Simon Peter motioned to him to ask Jesus of whom he was speaking. ²⁵ So that disciple, leaning back against Jesus, said to him, "Lord, who is it?" ²⁶ Jesus answered, "It is he to whom I will give this morsel of bread when I have dipped it." So when he had dipped the morsel, he gave it to Judas, the son of Simon Iscariot. ²⁷ Then after he had taken the morsel, Satan entered into him. Jesus said to him, "What you are going to do, do quickly."²⁸ Now no one at the table knew why he said this to him. ²⁹ Some thought that, because Judas had the moneybag, Jesus was telling him, "Buy what we need for the feast," or that he should give something to the poor. ³⁰ So, after receiving the morsel of bread, he immediately went out. And it was night.

MATTHEW 16:14-16

¹⁴ And they said, "Some say John the Baptist, others say Elijah, and others Jeremiah or one of the prophets." ¹⁵ He said to them, "But who do you say that I am?" ¹⁶ Simon Peter replied, "You are the Christ, the Son of the living God."

MATTHEW 27:5-7

[5] And throwing down the pieces of silver into the temple, he departed, and he went and hanged himself. [6] But the chief priests, taking the pieces of silver, said, "It is not lawful to put them into the treasury, since it is blood money." [7] So they took counsel and bought with them the potter's field as a burial place for strangers.

FRIDAY

ROMANS 3:23

[23] for all have sinned and fall short of the glory of God

ROMANS 5:8

[8] but God shows his love for us in that while we were still sinners, Christ died for us.

ROMANS 10:9

[9] because, if you confess with your mouth that Jesus is Lord and believe in your heart that God raised him from the dead, you will be saved.

Monday

READ: John 6:1-14

SOAP: John 6:5-7

Scripture - Write out the **Scripture** passage for the day.

Observations - Write down 1 or 2 **observations** from the passage.

Monday

Applications - Write down 1 or 2 **applications** from the passage.

Pray - Write out a **prayer** over what you learned from today's passage.

-Visit our website today for the corresponding blog post!-

Tuesday

READ: Philippians 4:19; Matthew 19:26

SOAP: Phil. 4:19; Matthew 19:26

Scripture - Write out the **Scripture** passage for the day.

Observations - Write down 1 or 2 **observations** from the passage.

Tuesday

Applications - Write down 1 or 2 **applications** from the passage.

Pray - Write out a **prayer** over what you learned from today's passage.

Wednesday

READ: John 14:8-9; 10:30
SOAP: John 14:8-9; 10:30

Scripture - Write out the **Scripture** passage for the day.

Observations - Write down 1 or 2 **observations** from the passage.

Wednesday

Applications - Write down 1 or 2 **applications** from the passage.

Pray - Write out a **prayer** over what you learned from today's passage.

-Visit our website today for the corresponding blog post!-

Thursday

READ: John 13:21-30; Matthew 16:14-16; 27:5-7

SOAP: Matthew 16:14-16

Scripture - Write out the **Scripture** passage for the day.

Observations - Write down 1 or 2 **observations** from the passage.

Thursday

Applications - Write down 1 or 2 **applications** from the passage.

Pray - Write out a **prayer** over what you learned from today's passage.

Friday

READ: Romans 3:23; 5:8; 10:9
SOAP: Romans 3:23; 5:8; 10:9

Scripture - Write out the **Scripture** passage for the day.

Observations - Write down 1 or 2 **observations** from the passage.

Friday

Applications - Write down 1 or 2 **applications** from the passage.

Pray - Write out a **prayer** over what you learned from today's passage.

-Visit our website today for the corresponding blog post!-

Reflection Questions

1. In what way was Jesus trying to test Philip?

2. Philip did not understand that with God all things are possible. When are you tempted to forget this important truth?

3. What truth about who Jesus is did Philip not understand?

4. What was Judas's first love? Why do you think Judas killed himself?

5. God calls everyone to repent and follow him. What happens when we do this? Is there any sin God is not willing to forgive? What hope does this give you?

My Response

Know these truths from God's Word...

God loves you.

Even when you're feeling unworthy and like the world is stacked against you, God loves you - *yes, you* - and He has created you for great purpose.

God's Word says, "God so loved the world that He gave His one and only Son, Jesus, that whoever believes in Him shall not perish, but have eternal life" (John 3:16).

Our sin separates us from God.

We are all sinners by nature and by choice, and because of this we are separated from God, who is holy.

God's Word says, "All have sinned and fall short of the glory of God" (Romans 3:23).

Jesus died so that you might have life.

The consequence of sin is death, but your story doesn't have to end there! God's free gift of salvation is available to us because Jesus took the penalty for our sin when He died on the cross.

God's Word says, "For the wages of sin is death, but the free gift of

God is eternal life in Christ Jesus our Lord" (Romans 6:23); "God demonstrates His own love toward us, in that while we were yet sinners, Christ died for us" (Romans 5:8).

Jesus lives!

Death could not hold Him, and three days after His body was placed in the tomb Jesus rose again, defeating sin and death forever! He lives today in heaven and is preparing a place in eternity for all who believe in Him.

> God's Word says, "In my Father's house are many rooms. If it were not so, would I have told you that I go to prepare a place for you? And if I go and prepare a place for you, I will come again and will take you to myself, that where I am you may be also" (John 14:2-3).

Yes, you can KNOW that you are forgiven.

Accept Jesus as the only way to salvation…

Accepting Jesus as your Savior is not about what you can do, but rather about having faith in what Jesus has already done. It takes recognizing that you are a sinner, believing that Jesus died for your sins, and asking for forgiveness by placing your full trust in Jesus's work on the cross on your behalf.

> God's Word says, "If you confess with your mouth that Jesus is Lord and believe in your heart that God raised him from the dead, you will be saved. For with the heart one believes and is justified, and with the mouth one confesses and is saved" (Romans 10:9-10).

Practically, what does that look like? With a sincere heart, you can pray a simple prayer like this:

God,

I know that I am a sinner.

I don't want to live another day without embracing

the love and forgiveness that You have for me.

I ask for Your forgiveness.

I believe that You died for my sins and rose from the dead.

I surrender all that I am and ask You to be Lord of my life.

Help me to turn from my sin and follow You.

Teach me what it means to walk in freedom as I live under Your grace,

and help me to grow in Your ways as I seek to know You more.

Amen.

If you just prayed this prayer (or something similar in your own words), would you email us at info@lovegodgreatly.com? We'd love to help get you started on this exciting journey as a child of God!

a LoveGodGreatly Bible Study Journal

David

HIS STORY IS OUR STORY

293

Welcome, friend. We're so glad you're here...

LOVE GOD GREATLY exists to inspire, encourage, and equip women all over the world to make God's Word a priority in their lives.

-INSPIRE-

women to make God's Word a priority in their daily lives through our Bible study resources.

-ENCOURAGE-

women in their daily walks with God through online community and personal accountability.

-EQUIP-

women to grow in their faith, so that they can effectively reach others for Christ.

Love God Greatly consists of a beautiful community of women who use a variety of technology platforms to keep each other accountable in God's Word.

We start with a simple Bible reading plan, but it doesn't stop there.

Some gather in homes and churches locally, while others connect online with women across the globe. Whatever the method, we lovingly lock arms and unite for this purpose...

to Love God Greatly with our lives.

At *Love God Greatly*, you'll find real, authentic women. Women who are imperfect, yet forgiven. Women who desire less of us, and a whole lot more of Jesus. Women who long to know God through his Word, because we know that Truth transforms and sets us free. ***Women who are better together, saturated in God's Word and in community with one another.***

Love God Greatly is a 501 (C) (3) non-profit organization. Funding for Love God Greatly comes through donations and proceeds from our online Bible study journals and books. LGG is committed to providing quality Bible study materials and believes finances should never get in the way of a woman being able to participate in one of our studies. All LGG journals and translated journals are available to download for free from LoveGodGreatly.com for those who cannot afford to purchase them. Our journals and books are also available for sale on Amazon. Search for "Love God Greatly" to see all of our Bible study journals and books. 100% of proceeds go directly back into supporting Love God Greatly and helping us inspire, encourage and equip women all over the world with God's Word.

THANK YOU for partnering with us!

What we offer:

18 + Translations | Bible Reading Plans | Online Bible Study
Love God Greatly App | 80 + Countries Served
Bible Study Journals & Books | Community Groups

Each Love God Greatly study includes:

Three Devotional Corresponding Blog Posts | Monday Vlog Videos
Memory Verses | Weekly Challenge | Weekly Reading Plan
Reflection Questions And More!

Other Love God Greatly studies include:

David | Ecclesiastes | Growing Through Prayer | Names Of God
Galatians | Psalm 119 | 1st & 2nd Peter | Made For Community | Esther
The Road To Christmas | The Source Of Gratitude | You Are Loved

YOU CAN FIND US ONLINE AT LOVEGODGREATLY.COM